The Singular Life of
Albert Nobbs

ALMA CLASSICS LTD
London House
243-253 Lower Mortlake Road
Richmond
Surrey TW9 2LL
United Kingdom
www.almaclassics.com

The Singular Life of Albert Nobbs first published in French in 1977
This translation first published by John Calder (Publishers) Ltd in 1979
This edition first published by Alma Classics Ltd in 2012

© Les Éditions des Femmes, 1977
Translation © John Calder (Publishers) Ltd, 1979

Printed in Great Britain by CPI Group (UK) Ltd, Croydon CR0 4YY

Typeset by Tetragon

ISBN: 978-1-84749-553-2

The Singular Life of Albert Nobbs

Simone Benmussa

Adapted for the stage from
George Moore's short story 'Albert Nobbs'

Translated by Barbara Wright

ALMA CLASSICS

Introduction

The costumes in *The Singular Life of Albert Nobbs* have a role, just as the actors do. They do not merely function as decoration or historical reconstitution, they are more than that. They are an intrinsic part of the text, of the gestures, and even of the scenic writing: they are the necessary point of departure for the expression of the other themes. All the characters wear professional clothes; even Mrs Baker is dressed as the bourgeois proprietress of a hotel. For the maids, for Nobbs, as well as for the prostitute, their clothes represent the force of work in society. Albert had picked out an evening suit from a bundle of old clothes that her former master, Mr Congreve, had given her to sell. Dressed in these evening clothes disguised as a man, Albert was able to get a job in a big restaurant as an "extra" waiter, and so be better paid. The beloved master's suit becomes that of the manservant, hence it fulfils various functions, according to whether there is a white apron over it or not. The ambiguity of Nobbs's situation is thus registered from the start. She wears the costume of the only person she could have loved, but she thereby puts herself in the position of never being able to be loved by any man. Dressed thus, she becomes the master of the maidservants, and so has a place of authority in the hierarchy of the hotel workers, but she feels the marginality of her situation, because she is the only person who knows that she has become a "perhapser". Her costume must be strict and plain, black and white. She is imprisoned in this costume, which is at the same time armour, yoke and defence. Her costume has become her body. This was the starting point from which I directed the actresses. Nobbs's shoes are important too: big men's shoes which anchor her to the ground, give her weight. I had to expose the scandal that a woman's body hidden under this man's body represents for society. While it was only an accident that Albert first wore this costume, in order to get work, or in her own defence, there was a possibility that the same costume might provide her with something other than work, might become her means of subsistence and survival – but would it do so? For at the same time it exiled her for life from her own body.

In contrast, the costume of Hubert Page, herself a woman disguised as a man in order to be able to work, is supple and loose: she wears a painter's smock. There is something free and informal about this costume. Hubert Page is the mistress of her own actions; it was she who decided to work as a man: she had already helped her husband in this way, she decided to leave home, to join fortunes with another woman, she is a house-painter, has no place in any hierarchy, and is happy. At the end of the play, though, in order not to die like Albert, suffocated by her secret, she goes back home. In this play, costume is the pivot between life and death.

Albert Nobbs poses the problem of disguise, but breaks with the theatrical tradition of travesty. Plays on the theme of travesty are centred round revelation, unmasking, as in Shakespeare, for instance, or in *Der Rosenkavalier*. There is always something temporary – a plot, a strategy triumphed over by the person who adopts the disguise, whereas in *Albert Nobbs*, it is her destiny. Starting as her refuge from society, this disguise becomes her prison, and then her grave. In the same way, the money she accumulates to give herself security, to bring her happiness, becomes her obsession. She wraps it in pink or blue paper, she makes little packets of it, she parcels up this body/money, she hides it under the floor, which is the grave; she buries it as she buries herself under her disguise.

This difference between travesty (a changed body) and disguise (a hidden body) is of great importance to the way the actress plays her part. Albert doesn't fantasize. She has no fantasies about the inversion of the sexual roles. No: I see no sexual problems in Nobbs, but a kind of pursuit of happiness, a kind of reverie, a very logical, systematic and deductive reverie. She does her accounts. She has the simplicity to be able to add up. What she is looking for is a house, for want of a body. For her, the image of happiness lies in the bourgeoisie in which she has served: this is the only model she has.

When I was working on the adaptation of this short story, what I appreciated was the force, the simplicity, the obviousness, the incredibility of this true story which, starting from a simple, naive news item, became the expression of an extremely transgressive political situation – and this without being in any way didactic. Through it, I saw the other themes we could bring out: discrimination, women's work, the situation of the "perhapser", solitude, marginality, bastardy, the adventure of marriage as a community of interests and not as a sexual adventure – which I found extremely modern for those days – and celibacy. In the course of the adaptation, everything changes: one ransacks the text, one creates one's own reverie, one follows the subterranean layers of one's own imagination and of one's own fantasies. One discovers different things. When archeologists start their digs, under a Romanesque basilica they may find a Greek or Roman temple, below that a Punic temple, and so on. The different periods are often superimposed, and contradictory. And though I considered that Moore had told this story with a great deal of respect, tenderness and humour, while I was working on it I realized that on the one hand he saw things from the point of view of a man telling a woman's story (his humour was tinged with irony), and that on the other hand he saw things from a writer's point of view – that's to say with the writer's inevitable distance from the characters who are the subject of the narrative, whereas on stage the characters are no longer described: they are living. And as I became more deeply involved, I came to see things from an entirely personal and feminine viewpoint, which was therefore nearer to this woman, Albert Nobbs, nearer to the everyday objects that surround her, nearer to her familiar decor. The tea tray Nobbs carries has the importance of a word; the way the actress carries it is the equivalent of a phrase. The doors that move of their own accord carry on a dialogue with the actors, as do the lights, the movements of a dress, or the folds of a coat. The images take form in this way, and create a new kind of writing.

The theme of the play is Albert's transgression in dressing as a man; she goes against the way in which society is ordered. In the same way, the structure of the play transgresses the established order of the theatre – it is as if the narrative were thwarted by the real life of the characters. The continual play between the distance implied by the narration, and on the other hand the identification with the characters demanded by the theatre, obliges this ubiquity to be both *there* and *elsewhere*, and at the same time creates a conflict which on the one hand shatters the habitual structures of the theatre, and on the other hand shatters the traditional structures of the narrative form. In this way a new rhythm is created which is the opposite of the illustrative theatre, or of simple distancing. The actor is playing on two levels, then: the acting must be extremely real and simple (without ever becoming realistic; in other words, deprived of all theatricality), but it must also contain moments of unreality, just as in music, the scale of C is broken up by sharps and flats.

In the course of rehearsal, Moore became a character like all the others; with his "voice off", he is living his life in the same way as the rest of them. The actresses had to act with these voices and bring them to life, as if the unreal were a concrete part of everyday life – which is a fact.

This unreality must be suggested. The stage speaks very loudly and very rapidly; a stage image is immediately striking, and as the audience cannot go back and reread, as they could with a book, the slightest nuance must be visible. To succeed in conveying what is merely suggested, we have to go very far, into the farthest distance, into the most delicate, the most secret recesses of the characters and of the space that surrounds and penetrates them, which they in their turn must haunt. For example, the movements of the two maidservants round Nobbs and Helen Dawes enabled us to convey Nobbs's unspoken, interior impressions. Her feminine reality beneath her man's clothes was displaced and taken over by their continual presence. They were her feminine doubles. From the moment when she puts aside her first sovereign for the purchase of a clock, and as we watch the unfolding of her reverie about the possibility of building happiness for herself – which would mean the rediscovery of her own being – her feminine body becomes materialized in the maidservants. The woman in her transpires, emerges, is "represented" behind her, beside her, around her, as the maidservants, going about their work, make feminine gestures. The woman in her cannot emerge in the professional milieu she is caught up in, in that Victorian paternalism which alienates her, although she thought she was being protected. One more disguise.

Even Moore, a man who felt a certain tenderness towards this story, displayed a kind of violence towards Nobbs. Ought I to have conformed to the casting that the story seemed to prescribe? A masculine-type woman, ugly, gaunt, about fifty, with yellow teeth, etc.? Had I done so, I should have been conforming to the idea of the whole thing being comic, indecent, I should have fallen into the traps of plot and the *coup de théâtre*: "Ah! It's a woman!" In that case I should have been humiliated; really it humiliated me to think that Albert might have been called ugly and unlovable. I found it misogynous and trivializing that people would be able to say: "That sort of thing only happens to ugly women." I preferred to put together a young cast – to embody, that is, the interior of the characters, to embody the force of the transgression; it wasn't of the slightest importance whether Nobbs was beautiful or ugly. I preferred not to approach the question in the usual way, where, starting from their appearance, actors express the inner life of characters according to the theatre's psychological laws. I chose the opposite approach: starting from their interior life, to make their exterior body plausible. And here we come back to the problem raised by Nobbs: the costume makes the body believable. Neither Susannah York nor Juliet Berto was physically Nobbs; they made her plausible, though, by their acting, their costume, and their feeling for the imaginary. This is why I could not, either, do what Moore did and show Albert as a corpse – no, I just could not bring myself to do her that violence. Albert is there, sitting on her chair, the chair that has become far more than just her chair. It is her *place* – a place she has come to know by heart in all its details: its consistency, colour, polish and scratches. I could not take away her disguise when she was dead, as people "take away" a corpse from a house in order to bury it: only her hands, which had been polishing shoes, remain suspended in mid-air.

– Simone Benmussa

Stephanie Beecham as Hubert Page   *Photo: Lesly Hamilton*

Susannah York as Albert Nobbs

Photo: Lesly Hamilton

Julia Foster as Helen Dawes and Susannah York as Albert Nobbs at the New End,
Hampstead, 1978.   *Photo: Lesly Hamilton*

Susannah York as Albert Nobbs and Stephanie Beecham as Hubert Page.
                                                                   Photo: Lesly Hamilton

The Singular Life of
Albert Nobbs

The Singular Life of Albert Nobbs was first performed in
this translation at the New End Theatre on June 27th, 1978
with the following cast:

ALBERT NOBBS	Susannah York
HELEN DAWES	Julia Foster
HUBERT PAGE	Stephanie Beacham
MRS BAKER	Nan Munro
KITTY MacCAN	Veronica Duffy
1ST CHAMBER MAID	Maria Harper
2ND CHAMBER MAID	Fiona Reid
GEORGE MOORE'S VOICE	Allen McLelland
ALEC'S VOICE	Dermot Crowley
JOE MACKINS	Kevin Moore

Directed and designed by Simone Benmussa

Produced by Buddy Dalton and Richard Jackson

La vie singulière d'Albert Nobbs was first performed by
the Compagnie Renaud-Barrault at the Théâtre d'Orsay,
Paris, November 1977, directed by Simone Benmussa with
Juliet Berto as Albert Nobbs

Prologue

The house lights go out.

GEORGE MOORE'S VOICE: Good morning, Alec.

ALEC'S VOICE: Good morning, Your Honour.

GEORGE MOORE'S VOICE: And what story are you going to tell me today, Alec? Will it be as strange as the one about the hermit? Upon my word, there is nothing like the bank of a river for storytelling.

ALEC'S VOICE: 'Tis true that they seem to come swirling up from the river bed.

GEORGE MOORE'S VOICE: The old storytellers of Mayo, your ancestors, always looked for inspiration in running water.

ALEC'S VOICE: But it is your turn today, Your Honour.

GEORGE MOORE'S VOICE: So it is... Well then, I shall tell you a true story.

This takes place in the 1860s, in Ireland.

The voice of a drunken old Irishman can be heard in the distance, singing 'The Boys of the Column'. It fades away as GEORGE MOORE *begins his story.*

Two chambermaids, dressed identically in black dresses and long white aprons, gently pull back the curtains, just as they would draw bedroom curtains in the morning. They reveal the interior of a hotel: Morrison's Hotel. In the half-light it is just possible to make out: on one side, in the void, a swing door leading to the kitchen: its upper part is glass, its lower part wood. On the other side, equally isolated, a revolving wood-and-glass door such as are to be found in old hotels: this is the front door. The two doors will later revolve or swing of their own accord, the one opening on to the world of the kitchen, the other on to that of the clients, as if ghostly visitors or maids, fairies or voices, were passing through them.

GEORGE MOORE'S VOICE: When we went up to Dublin in the Sixties, Alec, we always put up at Morrison's, a big family hotel. I can still see Morrison's: the front door opening into a short passage, with some half-dozen steps leading up into the house, the glass doors of the coffee room showing through the dimness, and in front of the visitor a big staircase running up to the second landing. I remember long passages on the second landing, and halfway down these passages was the well. I don't know if it's right to speak of the well of a staircase, but I used to think of it as a well. A very big building was Morrison's Hotel, with passages running hither and thither, and little flights of stairs in all kinds of odd corners. I remember the pair of windows, their lace curtains and their rep curtains; I can remember myself looking through the pane, interested in the coal carts going by, the bell hitched onto the horse's collar jangling all the way down the street, the coalman himself sitting with his legs hanging over the shafts, looking up at the windows to see if he could spy out an order.

After the maids have attached the curtains to their loops, they walk backstage, each keeping to her own side. When they get to the doors they stop and look at each other through the glass. The doors swing gently, though no one has touched them.

The decor and the characters can just be made out on the dimly lit stage.

A backcloth: the different doors of the rooms on the upper floors, and the characters, taken from English paintings of the Victorian era. These are guests, maids, menservants, etc., painted in trompe l'oeil, *some going into the rooms, others carrying trays, maids leaning over the banisters looking down at the floor below, shoes waiting to be cleaned outside the closed doors. Some doors and windows can be opened to let the light through. In the middle of the staircase, halfway up, sitting on a chair but only just visible, a real character, a waiter, his napkin over his shoulder, as if he were an integral part of the centre of this backcloth, one of its painted characters. This is* ALBERT NOBBS.

The other characters are: MRS BAKER, *at her table, bending over her account book, and* HUBERT PAGE, *a house-painter, standing on a ladder.*

A child is looking out of one of the windows backstage. He has his back turned; he shuts the window, goes downstairs, crosses the stage and exits.

The lights come up.

The two "ghost-maids" are blinded by the light and disappear, as if the brightness has dissolved them into thin air.

The hotel comes to life.

The doors swing and revolve, carrying on a dialogue with each other.

GEORGE MOORE'S VOICE: I'm telling you these things, Alec, for the pleasure of looking back and nothing else. I can see the sitting room – and the waiter that used to attend on us, I can see him too. And to this day I can recall the frights he gave me when he came behind me, awaking me from my dream of a coalman's life. I used to be afraid to open the sitting-room door, for I'd be sure to find him waiting on the landing, his napkin thrown over his shoulder. I think I was afraid he'd pick me up and kiss me. And yet all the guests liked Albert Nobbs. And the proprietress liked him – as well she might – for he was the most dependable servant in the hotel: no running round to public-houses and coming back with the smell of whisky and tobacco upon him; no rank pipe in his pocket; and above all, no playing the fool with the maidservants. Holidays he never asked for. A strange life his was, and mysterious.

ALBERT NOBBS *gets up from his chair and goes over to an open window next to the one where the child had been. He leans out, just as the child had, and then comes down.* MRS BAKER *goes over to another window downstage, stays there a moment, leaning out like the child and* ALBERT NOBBS. HUBERT PAGE *comes down from his ladder and goes to put it and his brushes away. He reappears and passes* ALBERT NOBBS. *They gaze at each other.*

MRS BAKER *is standing in front of* ALBERT NOBBS, *looking amazed.* HUBERT *stops and glances from one to the other, surprised, smiling, embarrassed.* MRS BAKER *is both perplexed and displeased. It is as if they are frozen in their conversation – a conversation that has not yet taken place.*

ALEC'S VOICE: Why mysterious?

GEORGE MOORE'S VOICE: Because when he died, we learnt that Albert was a woman.

ALEC'S VOICE: A woman?

GEORGE MOORE'S VOICE: Yes, a woman, and Hubert Page too.

ALEC'S VOICE: I don't understand, Your Honour.

GEORGE MOORE'S VOICE: You soon will. His willingness to oblige was so notorious that Mrs Baker, the proprietress of Morrison's Hotel at the time, could hardly believe she was listening to him when he began to stumble from one excuse to another for not sharing his bed with Hubert Page. You see, Alec, it was Punchestown week, and beds are as scarce in Dublin that week as diamonds are on the slopes of Croagh Patrick.

ALEC'S VOICE: But Your Honour – you still haven't told me who Page was.

GEORGE MOORE'S VOICE: I'm just coming to him, Alec. Hubert Page was a house-painter, well known and well liked by Mrs Baker. He came over every season, and so pleasant were his manners that one forgot the smell of his paint.

A CHAMBERMAID'S VOICE: Good morning, Mr Page, what a pleasure to see you back at the hotel!

GEORGE MOORE'S VOICE: He went about his work with a sort of lolling, idle gait that attracted and pleased the eye.

MRS BAKER: I suppose you fully understand that Page is leaving for Belfast by the morning train, and has come over here to ask us for a bed, there not being one at the hotel in which he is working, nor in all Dublin.

GEORGE MOORE'S VOICE: Albert Nobbs understood well enough, but he began to mumble something about being a very light sleeper.

MRS BAKER: Now, what are you trying to say?

GEORGE MOORE'S VOICE: He complained that his mattress was full of lumps.

MRS BAKER: Your mattress full of lumps! Why, your mattress was repicked and buttoned six months ago. What kind of story are you telling me?

GEORGE MOORE'S VOICE: That he had never slept with anybody before, and that Mr Page would get a better stretch on one of the sofas in the coffee room.

MRS BAKER: A better stretch on the sofa in the coffee room? I don't understand you, not a little bit.

GEORGE MOORE'S VOICE: Page, for his part, said that the night was a fine one, that he would keep himself warm with a sharp walk, and that his train started early.

MRS BAKER: You'll do nothing of the kind, Page!

GEORGE MOORE'S VOICE: Seeing that Mrs Baker was now very angry, Albert thought it time to give in. You'll do nothing of the kind, Mr Page, he repeated.

MRS BAKER: I should think not indeed!

GEORGE MOORE'S VOICE: But I'm a light sleeper, he said again.

MRS BAKER: We've heard that before, Albert! (*Going out*) No inconvenience whatever, Page.

ALBERT NOBBS *goes over to a panel on which a sideboard and a pile of plates are painted in* trompe l'oeil. *She opens it. On the other side, her bedroom is painted. She pulls out a folding bed and sets it up, helped by*

HUBERT PAGE. HUBERT *is so dog-tired that he tumbles into bed, and a moment after is asleep.* ALBERT *stands listening, not yet undressed, his loosened tie dangling. When his heavy breathing tells* ALBERT *that* PAGE *is sound asleep, she approaches the bed stealthily. Relieved, she gets into bed, though she hasn't dared to undress completely. They sleep for a moment.*

THE FLEA

Suddenly ALBERT NOBBS *awakes with a start. A flea has bitten her, and out goes her leg. She is afraid that this lively movement has awoken* HUBERT PAGE, *but Hubert only turns over in the bed to sleep more soundly.* ALBERT *sits down cautiously on the bed, is reassured at seeing that* PAGE *is still asleep, and sets herself to the task of catching the flea. She lowers her shirt until one of her shoulders is naked. With her back to the audience, she starts scratching herself.*

This scene must be played with the greatest modesty and austerity, to enhance its innocence.

HUBERT PAGE: Why, you're a woman!

ALBERT NOBBS: You won't tell on me and ruin a poor man, will you, Mr Page? That is all I ask of you, and on my knees I beg it.

HUBERT PAGE: Get up from your knees. And tell me how long you have been playing this part?

ALBERT NOBBS: Ever since I was a girl. You won't tell on me, will you, Mr Page? You wouldn't prevent a poor woman from getting her living?

HUBERT PAGE: Not likely; but I'd like to hear how it all came about…

ALBERT NOBBS: How I went out as a youth to get my living?

HUBERT PAGE: Yes, tell me the story; for though I was very sleepy just now, the sleep has left my eyes and I'd like to hear it. But before you begin, tell me what you were doing, wriggling about like that.

ALBERT NOBBS: It was a flea. I suffer terribly from fleas, and you must have brought some in with you, Mr Page. I shall be covered in blotches in the morning.

HUBERT PAGE: I'm sorry for that. But tell me how long ago it was that you became a man? Before you came to Dublin, of course?

ALBERT NOBBS: Oh yes, long before…

HUBERT PAGE: Tell me…

ALBERT NOBBS: It is very cold.

HUBERT PAGE:… Come, tell me.

ALBERT NOBBS'S TALE

ALBERT NOBBS: You know I'm not Irish, Mr Page. My parents may have been, for all I know. The only one who knew who they were was my old nurse, and she never told me.

HUBERT PAGE: She never told you?

ALBERT NOBBS: No, she never told me, though I often asked her, saying no good would come of holding it back from me. She might have told me before she died, but she died suddenly.

HUBERT PAGE: Without telling you who you were!

ALBERT NOBBS: Yes.

HUBERT PAGE: You'd better begin at the beginning.

ALBERT NOBBS: The story seems to me to be without a beginning; anyway I don't know the beginning. I was a bastard. My old nurse hinted more than once that my people were grand folk, and I know she had a big allowance from them for my education. When they died, the allowance was no longer paid, and my nurse and myself had to go out to work. There was no time for picking and choosing. We hadn't what would keep us until the end of the month in the house... The first job that came our way was looking after chambers in the Temple. We had three gentlemen to look after, so there was eighteen shillings a week between my old nurse and myself; the omnibus fares had to come out of these wages, and to save sixpence a day we went to live in Temple Lane. (*Pause*) My old nurse didn't mind the lane; she had been a working woman all her life, but with me it was different. I got my education at a convent school, you know, and the change was so great from the convent that I often thought I would sooner die than continue to live like the animals, indecently – and life without decency is hardly bearable, so I thought. I've been through a great deal since in different hotels, and have become used to hard work. (*Pause*) And then my nurse's brother lost his post.

HUBERT PAGE: What did he do?

ALBERT NOBBS: He'd been a bandmaster, a bugler, or something to do with music in the country. He came to stay with us. My old nurse was obliged to give him sixpence a day, and the drop from eighteen shillings to fourteen and sixpence is a big one. My nurse worried about the food, but it was the rough men I worried about; the bandsman wouldn't leave me alone, and many's the time I've waited until the staircase was clear, afraid that if I met him or another I'd be caught hold of and held and pulled about. I might have been tempted if one of them had been less rough than the rest, and if I hadn't known I was a bastard; it was that, I think, that kept me straight more than anything else, for I had just begun to feel what a great misfortune it is for a poor girl to find herself in the family way; no greater misfortune can befall anyone in this world, but it would have been worse in my case, for I should only be bringing another bastard into the world.

HUBERT PAGE: But the gentlemen you worked for – were they at least pleasant?

ALBERT NOBBS: They were barristers, pleasant and considerate men they all were – yes, pleasant to work for. One of them was called Mr Congreve. He had chambers in Temple Gardens overlooking the river, and it was a pleasure to us to keep his pretty things clean, never breaking one of them. Looking back I can see that I must have loved Mr Congreve very dearly. (*Pause*) I can see him now as plainly as if he were before me – very thin and elegant, with long white hands. I used to know all his suits, as well I might, for it was my job to look after them, to brush them; and I used to spend a great deal more time than was needed taking out spots with benzine, arranging his neckties – he had fifty or sixty, all kinds – and seven or eight greatcoats. A real toff – my word, he was that, but not one of those haughty ones too proud to give one a nod. He always smiled and nodded if we met under the clock, he on his way to the library and I returning to Temple Lane. I used to look round after him saying: he's got on the striped trousers and the embroidered waistcoat.

HUBERT PAGE: Was there no woman in Mr Congreve's life?

ALBERT NOBBS: That was just it: I never found a hairpin in his bed. But one day, when I took him his letters, I said to myself: why, this one's from a woman. Nice, that's in France, I said to myself. And thought no more of the matter until another letter arrived from Nice. Now what can she be writing to him about, I wondered. Then a third letter arrived, and a box full of flowers. I can still see it. So overcome was I as I picked them up out of the box that a sudden faintness came over me, and my old nurse said: "What is the matter with thee?" Of course I never thought that Mr Congreve would look at me, and I don't know that I wanted him to, but I didn't want another woman about the place. I told myself that these rooms would be mine no longer. Of course they never were mine, but you know what I mean. A week later he said to me: There's a lady coming to lunchcon here, a French lady, and I remember the piercing that the words caused me, I can feel them here still. (ALBERT *puts her hand to her heart*) (*Pause*) Well, I had to serve the luncheon. (*Pause*) I'm sure no one ever suffered more than I did in those days. I don't think I ever hoped he'd fall in love with me. It wasn't as bad as that. It was the hopelessness of it that set the tears streaming down my cheeks. Mr Congreve's kindness seemed to hurt me more than anything. If only he'd spared me his kind words, and not spoken about the extra money he was going to give me for my attendance on his lady, I shouldn't have felt so much that they had lain side by side in the bed that I was making. I said to myself: I can't put up with it any longer. I began to think how I might make away with myself. I don't know if you know London, Hubert?

HUBERT PAGE: Of course I do, I'm a Londoner. I only come here to work every year.

ALBERT NOBBS: Then if you know the Temple, you know that the windows of Temple Gardens overlook the Thames. I often used to stand at those windows watching the big brown river flowing through its bridges, thinking all the while of the sea into which it went, and that I must plunge into the river and be carried away down to the sea, or be picked up before I got there. I could only think about making an end to my trouble and of the Frenchwoman. I'm sure if I hadn't met Bessie Lawrence I should have done away with myself.

HUBERT PAGE: Bessie Lawrence?

ALBERT NOBBS: She was the woman who used to look after the chambers under Mr Congreve's. We stopped talking outside the gateway by King's

Bench Walk – if you know the Temple, you know where I mean.

Simultaneously:

BESSIE'S VOICE: There is a big dinner at the Freemason's Tavern tonight, and they're short of waiters. If it wasn't for my hips and bosom I'd very soon be into a suit of evening clothes and getting ten shillings for the job. If only I had a figure like yours.

ALBERT NOBBS: Bessie kept on talking... but I wasn't listening... only catching a word here and there... not waking up from my dream how to make away with myself...

ALBERT NOBBS: My figure! – No one had ever spoken about my figure before – what had my figure got to do with it?

BESSIE'S VOICE: You haven't been listening to me.

Almost at the same time, but just slightly out of phase:

ALBERT NOBBS (*to* HUBERT): You haven't been listening to me, she said. I only missed the last few words.

BESSIE'S VOICE: Just missed the last few words?... You didn't hear me telling you that there is a big dinner at the Freemason's Tavern tonight, and they're short of waiters?

ALBERT NOBBS: But what has that got to do with my figure?

BESSIE'S VOICE: Didn't I say that if it wasn't for my hips and bosom I'd very soon be into a suit of evening clothes and getting ten shillings for the job?

ALBERT NOBBS: But what has that got to do with my figure?

BESSIE'S VOICE: Your figure is just the one for a waiter's.

ALBERT NOBBS: Oh, I'd never thought of that.

Mr Congreve had given me a bundle of old clothes to sell. A suit of evening clothes was in it. You see, Mr Congreve and myself were about the same height and build. The trousers will just want a bit of shortening, I said to myself, and I set to work; and at six o'clock I was in them and down at the Freemason's Tavern answering questions, saying that I had been accustomed to waiting tables. I was taken on, and it was a mess that I made of it, getting in everybody's way; but my awkwardness was taken in good part and I received the ten shillings, which was good money for the sort of work I did that night.

But what stood to me was not so much the ten shillings that I earned as the bit I had learned. It was only a bit, not much bigger than a threepenny bit, but I had worked round a table at a big dinner. The food I'd had, and the excitement of the dinner, the guests, the lights, the talk, stood to me, and things seemed clearer than they had ever seemed before.

Another job came along, and another and another. Each of these jobs was worth ten shillings to me, to say nothing of the learning of the trade; and having the making of a waiter in me, it didn't take more than about three months for me to be as quick and as smart and as watchful as the best of them, and without these qualities no one will succeed in waiting. I have worked round the tables in the biggest places in London and all over England in all the big towns – in Manchester, in Liverpool and Birmingham. It was seven years ago that I came here, and here it would seem that I've come to be looked on as a fixture, for the Bakers are good people to work for, and I may as well be here as elsewhere.

HUBERT PAGE: Seven years working in Morrison's Hotel, and on the second floor?

ALBERT NOBBS: Yes, the second floor is the best in the hotel; the money is better than in the coffee room, and that is why the Bakers have put me there. They've often said they don't know what they'd do without me.

HUBERT PAGE: Seven years, the same work up the stairs and down the stairs, banging into the kitchen and out again.

ALBERT NOBBS: There's more variety in the work than you think, Hubert. Every family is different, and so you're always learning.

HUBERT PAGE: Seven years! Neither man nor woman, just a perhapser.

HUBERT PAGE *had spoken these words more to himself than to* ALBERT NOBBS, *but feeling he had expressed himself incautiously he raised his eyes and read on* ALBERT's *face that the words had gone home, and that this outcast from both sexes felt her loneliness perhaps more keenly than before.*

ALBERT NOBBS: Neither man nor woman; yet nobody ever would have suspected me till the day of my death if it hadn't been for that flea that you brought in with you.

HUBERT PAGE: But what harm did the flea do you?

ALBERT NOBBS: I'm bitten all over.

HUBERT PAGE: Never mind the bites; we wouldn't have had this talk if it hadn't been for the flea, and I shouldn't have heard your story.

ALBERT NOBBS *tries to keep her tears back, but they are soon running quickly down her cheeks.*

ALBERT NOBBS: I thought nobody would ever hear it, and I thought I should never cry again.

It's all much sadder than I thought it was, and if I'd known how sad it was I shouldn't have been able to live through it. But I've jostled along somehow, always merry and bright, with never anyone to speak to, not really to speak to, only to ask for plates and dishes, for knives and forks and suchlike, tablecloths and napkins... It might have been better if I had taken the plunge.

She calms down.

But why am I thinking these things? It's you that has set me thinking, Hubert.

HUBERT PAGE: I'm sorry if...

ALBERT NOBBS: Oh, it's no use being sorry, and I'm a great silly to cry like this. I thought that regrets had passed away with the petticoats. But you've awakened the woman in me. You've brought it all up again. But I mustn't let on like this; it's very foolish of an old perhapser like me, neither man nor woman. But I can't help it. You understand... the loneliness...

She begins to sob again. HUBERT PAGE *waits until the paroxysm is over:*

HUBERT PAGE: Lonely, yes, I suppose it is lonely.

ALBERT NOBBS: You're very good, Mr Page, and I'm sure you'll keep my secret, though indeed I don't care very much whether you do or not.

HUBERT PAGE: Now, don't let on like that again. I'm sure it's lonely for you to live without man or without woman, thinking like a man and feeling like a woman.

ALBERT NOBBS: You seem to know all about it, Hubert. I hadn't thought of it like that before myself. You're quite right. I suppose I was wrong to put off my petticoats and step into those trousers.

HUBERT PAGE: I wouldn't got so far as to say that.

ALBERT NOBBS: Why do you say that, Hubert?

HUBERT PAGE: Well, because I was thinking that you might marry.

ALBERT NOBBS: But I was never a success as a girl. Men didn't look at me then, so I'm sure they wouldn't now that I'm a middle-aged woman. Marriage! Whom should I marry? No, there's no marriage for me in the world; I must go on being a man. But you won't tell on me? You've promised, Hubert.

HUPERT PAGE: Of course I won't tell, but I don't see why you shouldn't marry.

ALBERT NOBBS: What do you mean, Hubert? You aren't putting a joke upon me, are you? If you are, it's very unkind.

HUBERT PAGE: A joke upon you? Not at all. I didn't mean that you should marry a man, but you might marry a girl.

ALBERT NOBBS: Marry a girl?... a girl?

HUBERT PAGE: Well, anyway, that's what I've done.

ALBERT NOBBS: But you're a young man, and a very handsome young man too. Any girl would like to have you, and I dare say they were all after you before you met the right girl.

HUBERT PAGE: Listen to me, Albert. (*Pause*) I'm not a man.

ALBERT NOBBS: Ah! now I know for certain you're putting a joke upon me.

HUBERT PAGE: No, I'm not a man, I'm a woman.

They look at each other. The sincerity in ALBERT NOBBS'*s gaze gives* HUBERT PAGE *the courage to continue:*

My husband was a house-painter. After the birth of my second child he changed towards me altogether. He drank, he beat me, he left me without money for food, and sold up the home twice. At last I decided to have another cut at it, and catching sight of my husband's working clothes one day I said to myself: He's often made me put these on and go out and help him with his job; why shouldn't I put them on for myself and go away for good? It broke my heart to leave the children, but I couldn't remain with him.

ALBERT NOBBS: But the other marriage?

HUBERT PAGE: It was lonely going home to an empty room; I was as lonely as you, and one day, meeting a girl as lonely as myself, I said: "Come along," and we arranged to live together, each paying our share. She had her work and I had mine, and between us we made a fair living; and this I can say with truth: that we haven't known an unhappy hour since we married. People began to talk, so we had to. I'd like you to see our home. I always return to my home after a job is finished with a light heart and leave it with a heavy one.

ALBERT NOBBS: But I don't understand.

HUBERT PAGE: What don't you understand? It's very simple.

ALBERT NOBBS: I can't think now of what I was going to ask you...

HUBERT PAGE: You're falling asleep, and I'm doing the same. It must be three o'clock in the morning and I've to catch the five o'clock train.

ALBERT NOBBS: But you'll tell me later...

HUBERT PAGE: Yes, got to sleep now. I'll tell you later.

ALBERT NOBBS *remains sitting on the bed, motionless.*

HUBERT PAGE *gets up, looks through the windows at the dawn rising and steals away very quietly, while* ALBERT *lies down and falls asleep.*

It is morning. HUBERT PAGE *has gone.* ALBERT NOBBS *is alone in her bed.*

ALBERT NOBBS: His train started from Amiens Street at... I must have slept heavily for him – for her not to have awakened me, or she must have stolen away very quietly. But I mustn't fall into the habit of she-ing him. Lord amassy, what time is it?

She looks at the time and jumps out of bed. Folds it. Dresses...

An hour late... Such a thing never happened to me before. And the hotel as full as it can hold. Why didn't they send for me? Lord, if the missis knew everything! But I've overslept myself a full hour. The greater haste the less speed.

ALBERT NOBBS *puts her bed away and, still dressing, runs out onto her landing. The swing door comes into operation. Bedroom bells can be heard, and the voices of maids and cooks.* ALBERT *gets into her apron, laces her shoes, buttons her waistcoat, puts on her jacket, etc…*

ALBERT NOBBS: We're late today, and the house full of visitors.

A VOICE: 54 has just rung, Albert.

MRS BAKER: How is it that 54 isn't turned out? Has 35 rung his bell?

ALBERT NOBBS: Not yet, Mrs Baker.

A COOK'S VOICE: 22 and 12 want their breakfasts.

ANOTHER COOK'S VOICE: Fried or boiled egg for 22?

ALBERT NOBBS *is surrounded by all these voices. She stops, and seems to be thinking, dreaming. It isn't clear whether the voices are her real, everyday noises, or those she heard during the night, or the result of her fatigue…*

A VOICE: Sitting up half the night talking to Mr Page, and then rounding on us.

She is tying her tie.

ALBERT NOBBS: Half the night talking! Where is Mr Page? I didn't hear him go away; he may have missed his train for aught I know. But do get on with your work, and let me be getting on with mine.

ANOTHER VOICE: You're very cross this morning, Albert.

THE HEAD PORTER'S VOICE: Well, Mr Nobbs, how did you find your bedfellow?

ALBERT NOBBS: Oh, he was all right, but I'm not used to bedfellows, and he brought a flea with him, and it kept me awake. When I did fall asleep, I slept so heavily that I was an hour late. I hope he caught his train.

ALBERT NOBBS *goes up to her landing and takes her seat in the passage, her napkin over her shoulder. She asks herself, anxiously:*

ALBERT NOBBS: But what is all this pother about bedfellows?

Enter MRS BAKER. *She sits down at her work table.*

The hotel has calmed down. The light in the windows changes; the morning suns turns into that of the late afternoon. It is as if time is standing still at the beginning of the evening. ALBERT *speaks in a monologue with three voices: her inner voice and that of* GEORGE MOORE *come from somewhere quite different. A soft light, with occasional patches of semi-darkness.*

ALBERT'S DREAM

ALBERT NOBBS: Page hasn't said anything – no, she's said nothing, for we are both in the same boat, and to tell on me would be to tell on herself. (*Pause*) She's a woman right enough. But the cheek of it, to marry an innocent girl! Did she let the girl into the secret, or leave her to find it out when... The girl might have called in the police!

GEORGE MOORE'S VOICE: This was a question one might ponder on. She wouldn't have had the cheek to wed her, Albert said to herself, without warning her that things might not turn out as she fancied.

ALBERT NOBBS: Maybe she didn't tell her before they wedded, and maybe she did.

MRS BAKER *passes, on her way to the bedrooms on the first floor.*

MRS BAKER: Were you speaking to me, Albert?

ALBERT NOBBS (*starting up from her chair guiltily, as if woken out of a dream*): No no, Mrs Baker, I didn't say anything.

MRS BAKER: Did you sleep well last night then, Albert?

ALBERT: Yes thank you, Mrs Baker, I only just awoke from time to time...

She goes and sits down. At MRS BAKER*'s next order she jumps up again like a puppet.*

27

MRS BAKER: Don't forget 35's tea.

MRS BAKER *disappears behind a door.* ALBERT NOBBS *goes back to her reverie. She walks up and down slowly, keeping time with her thoughts.*

ALBERT NOBBS: Right away, Mrs Baker.

ALBERT NOBBS *comes down from her landing, walks slowly over to the kitchen to fetch a tea tray and comes back. She is so lost in her thoughts that she has forgotten where she was supposed to take the tray, and goes back to the kitchen with it.*

ALBERT NOBBS: But Hubert did say that she had lived with a girl first, and wedded her to put a stop to people's scandal. Of course they could hardly live together except as man and wife. She always returned home with a light heart and never left it without a heavy one.

So it would seem that this marriage was as successful as any, and a great deal more than most.

The light changes. It is evening. The gas lamps come on. The backcloth seems to come to life. A guest, whom we don't see, comes downstairs. She passes by, and goes out of the hotel through the revolving door, which rotates of its own accord. The very real MRS BAKER *follows the guest.*

THE GUEST'S VOICE: Have a good evening, Albert; we're off to the theatre.

ALBERT NOBBS: Have a good evening, Mrs Lavery. I'm sure it will be an interesting play.

MRS BAKER: Albert, I'm going out; I'm leaving you in charge of the hotel.

ALBERT NOBBS: Have no fear, Mrs Baker.

ALBERT NOBBS *goes back to her reverie, and automatically makes her way up to her chair again.*

Hubert married.

Of course it wasn't a real marriage, it couldn't be that.

But a very happy one it would seem. (*Pause*)

For after all I've worked hard... Five-and-twenty years... a mere drifting from one hotel to another, without friends.

A housemaid, ALBERT NOBBS's *double, her feminine counterpart, appears behind Albert... follows her, helps her and accompanies her in her reverie.* ALBERT *goes and picks up a pair of shoes left outside a door and returns to her chair. Her feminine double hands her the duster and brush.*

ALBERT NOBBS: But what if Hubert was putting a joke upon me? (*Pause*)

I didn't ask her what her home might be like. I should have asked if she had a clock and vases on the chimney-piece.

Voice of a maid calling from the end of the passage.

VOICE: Albert!

ALBERT NOBBS: Coming.

THE VOICE: 54 wants his bottle of mineral water.

ALBERT NOBBS *stands up, puts down the shoes, goes into the kitchen and comes back with a bottle of mineral water on a tray. She takes it through one of the doors and comes and sits down again in her place. During this time the fairy-housemaid, her double, has been cleaning the shoes, and when* ALBERT *picks them up they are already beautifully polished.*

ALBERT NOBBS: It seems to me that Hubert said that her wife was a milliner. She may not have spoken the word milliner; but if she hadn't, it is strange that the word should keep on coming up in my mind. There is no reason why the wife shouldn't be a milliner, and if that is so it is as likely as not that they own a house in some quiet, insignificant street, letting the dining room, back room and kitchen to a widow or to a pair of widows. The drawing room would be the workroom and showroom.

GEORGE MOORE'S VOICE: On second thoughts it seemed to Albert that if the business were millinery, it might be that Mrs Page would prefer the ground floor for her showroom.

ALBERT NOBBS: Or rather, they would have kept the whole of the ground floor and only let the rooms above. No, that would have meant that the widows would have had to go through their part of the house. That's always annoying. No lodgers at all. (*Pause*)

Her feminine double imitates every movement she makes. It is as if they are superimposed on each other.

On further thoughts, not a milliner but a seamstress... A small dressmaker's business in a quiet street would be in keeping with all Hubert said about her home.

I'm not sure, however, that if I found a girl willing to share her life with me it would be a seamstress's business I would be on the lookout for... I rather think that a sweet shop, newspapers and tobacco, would be my choice.

Why shouldn't I make a fresh start? Hubert had no difficulties.

ALBERT NOBBS'S VOICE: She said:

ALBERT NOBBS: I can recall her very words.

ALBERT NOBBS'S VOICE: I didn't mean you should marry a man, but a girl.

ALBERT NOBBS: I've saved – oh! how I've tried to save, for I don't wish to end my days in the workhouse... upwards of five hundred pounds, which is enough to purchase a little business...

GEORGE MOORE'S VOICE: If it took her two years to find a partner and a business, she would have at least seventy or eighty pounds more, which would be a great help, for it would be a mistake to put one's money into a falling business.

ALBERT NOBBS: If I found a partner, I'd have to do like Hubert, for marriage would put a stop to all tittle-tattle. I would be able to keep my place at Morrison's Hotel, or perhaps leave Morrison's and rely on jobs with my connections – it would be a case of picking and choosing the best: ten and sixpence a night, nothing under.

ALBERT NOBBS'S VOICE: I could make a round: Belfast, Liverpool, Manchester, Bradford... and after a month's absence, a couple of months maybe, I would return home, my heart anticipating a welcome – a real welcome, for though I would continue to be a man to the world, I would be a woman to the dear one at home.

She goes and puts the shoes down outside a bedroom door. Her double remains standing behind her chair.

ALBERT NOBBS: With a real partner, one whose heart is in the business, we might make as much as two hundred pounds a year – four pounds a week! And with four pounds a week our home would be as pretty and happy as any in the city of Dublin.

GEORGE MOORE'S VOICE: Two rooms and a kitchen were what she foresaw. The furniture began to creep into her imagination little by little. A large sofa by the fireplace covered with a chintz!

ALBERT NOBBS: But chintz dirties quickly in the city.

GEORGE MOORE'S VOICE: A dark velvet sofa might be more suitable.

ALBERT NOBBS: It will cost a great deal of money, five or six pounds; and at that rate fifty pounds won't go very far, for we must have a fine mattress; and if we are going to do things in that style, the home will cost us something like eighty pounds.

GEORGE MOORE'S VOICE: With luck, these eighty pounds could be earned within the next two years at Morrison's Hotel.

ALBERT NOBBS: The people in 34 are leaving tomorrow; they are always good for half a sovereign... tomorrow's half-sovereign must be put aside as the beginning of a sum of money for the purchase of a clock to stand on a marble chimney-piece or a mahogany chiffonier.

THE CONCERT

Enter MRS BAKER, *coming from the kitchen, followed by the second housemaid. The first housemaid comes down the stairs, fetches two chairs and puts them down with their backs to the audience.* MRS BAKER *and the first housemaid sit down on them, ready for the concert. The first housemaid's movements are rapid and unreal.* ALBERT NOBBS *is about to go upstairs.*

MRS BAKER: What can Albert be dreaming of? Albert, you took the drinks to 5 yesterday, but you forgot the cigars.

ALBERT NOBBS *turns round like a sleepwalker and goes upstairs.*

ALBERT NOBBS'S VOICE: A shop with two counters, one for cigars, tobacco, pipes and matches, and the other for all kinds of sweets.

MRS BAKER (*continuing a conversation with* THE HOUSEMAID): Morton asked her whether she loved him as much as she had loved Ralph. That was quite different. He was very good to me, she said. Do you think I won't be good to you? said Morton. If you loved me, you wouldn't kiss me like that – just a little peck. I don't know how to kiss any other way, she replied. This is the first time we have walked out together. I have never been out so late with a man. You can't love me, you only met me yesterday. But I am going to love you. Let me kiss you, that's the only way, he said. I would like a man to love me before he kissed me. Then you will never be loved, for it is by way of the lips that love enters into the blood, and so on and so forth – she was twisting him round her little finger.

THE HOUSEMAID: She was leading him on.

ALBERT NOBBS *comes down with two suitcases, following an invisible guest.*

THE GUEST'S VOICE: I'm sorry to disturb you, Mrs Baker, but I'm leaving now, the carriage is at the door.

MRS BAKER (*to the gentleman, whom we still cannot see*): Goodbye, Mr Ruttledge. What a pity you will not be at the concert. We shall see you next season, I hope.

THE GUEST'S VOICE: No doubt about that, Mrs Baker.

He laughs rather stupidly. Mrs Baker does the same, and waves goodbye to him. The revolving door rotates of its own accord as the invisible guest passes through it.

MRS BAKER: Goodbye, have a good journey!

THE GUEST'S VOICE: Goodbye, and thank you.

During this exchange of courtesies, ALBERT'*s thoughts are far away. She puts the luggage into the carriage automatically. She comes back and we see her in the doorway, holding out her hand, coming to life and bowing when she is given her tip. The carriage can be heard leaving.*

ALBERT NOBBS'S VOICE: A sovereign! That's good for a pair of pretty candlesticks and a round mirror.

Meanwhile, the first housemaid has brought in an easel, and then a picture which she places on the easel, in front of MRS BAKER. *The picture shows a lady singing and another accompanying her at the piano. This is the concert.*

MRS BAKER: Oh, I was forgetting: are you there, Albert?

ALBERT *comes back.*

Mrs Swift left me a crown for you.

ALBERT NOBBS: Thank you, Madam.

GEORGE MOORE'S VOICE: This unexpected crown set her pondering on the colour of the curtains in their sitting room.

The concert begins. During this scene, GEORGE MOORE's *and* ALBERT NOBBS's *voices are heard. Music: the Irish song: 'I once loved a boy'.*

GEORGE MOORE'S VOICE: Albert became suddenly conscious that a change had come into her life: the show was the same, but behind the show a new life was springing up, a strangely personal life. She wasn't as good a servant as heretofore. She knew it. Certain absences of mind, that was all.

The lights in the hotel go down.

ALBERT NOBBS: A widow with a child of three or four, a boy the son of a dead man. No, a woman who had been deserted before the birth of her child. I should be the father in everybody's eyes, except the mother's of course. (*Pause*) A babe that would come into the world some three or four months after our marriage, a little girl. What matter whether she calls me father or mother? They are but mere words that the lips speak, but love is in the heart, and only love matters. (*Pause*)

Some revivalist meetings are soon going to be held in Dublin. Many of our girls *attend* them, and an unlucky girl will be in luck's way if we should run across one another.

The concert ends.

MRS BAKER: Now whatever can Albert be brooding?

Voices of maidservants, chambermaids, floor waiters and cooks. The swing door swings of its own accord; the hotel is at its busiest. MRS BAKER *goes into the kitchens. The first housemaid removes the concert: the easel and picture. The second housemaid puts away the chairs.*

HOUSEMAIDS' VOICES (*whispered*): –Brooding a love-story?

–Not likely.

–A marriage with some girl outside? He isn't over-partial to any of us.

–Have you noticed that he is eager to avail himself of every excuse to absent himself from duty in the hotel?

–I have seen him in the smaller streets looking up at the houses.

–They say he has saved a good deal of money, and some of his savings are in house property.

–What would you say if Albert was going to be married, and was looking out for a house for his wife?

–He's been seen talking with Annie Watts.

These voices are mainly coming from the kitchen and are very audible every time the swing door opens.

MRS BAKER: Quiet, please! Less talk and more work!

The hotel calms down. The lights dim. Three chambermaids sing 'The Butcher's Boy'.

ALBERT NOBBS: Annie Watts? No, not she. After all, she is not in the family way, and her heart is not in her work. That isn't the sort for a shop. Whereas Dorothy Keyes is a glutton for work, but I couldn't abide that tall, angular woman with a neck like a swan's. And her manner is abrupt. While Alice's small, neat figure and quick intelligence mark her out for the job... But alas! Alice is hot-tempered. We should quarrel.

She picks up her napkin, which had slipped from her knee to the floor, and puts it back on her shoulder.

What about the maids on the floor above? Mary O'Brien would make an attractive shopwoman... she has a certain stateliness of figure and also of gait. Ah! but she's a Papist. And the experience of Irish Protestants show that Papists and Protestants don't mix.

A CHAMBERMAID'S VOICE: Is that the new one?

This remark vaguely interrupts ALBERT NOBBS's *musing.*

ALBERT NOBBS: There's that lazy girl Annie Watts, on the lookout for an excuse to chatter the time away instead of being about her work.

ALBERT NOBBS *goes over towards the kitchens and holds the swing door open. She speaks to* ANNIE WATTS, *whom he cannot see.*

ANNIE WATTS'S VOICE: Helen Dawes has arrived, Mr Albert – the new kitchen-maid.

ALBERT NOBBS: Ah!

ANNIE WATTS'S VOICE: She must be here.

She almost bumps into a girl coming through the swing doors: HELEN DAWES.

THE MEETING WITH HELEN DAWES

ANNIE WATTS'S VOICE: She is not at all what I had imagined.

ALBERT NOBBS: So you're the new one – Helen Dawes?

HELEN DAWES: I am indeed, sir.

HELEN DAWES *doesn't move.* ALBERT NOBBS *walks away, then half-turns back, looking at* HELEN *over her shoulder. The lights dim a little. They are quite a distance from each other, and remain motionless during the following speeches.*

ALEC'S VOICE: She has white, even teeth, Your Honour.

GEORGE MOORE'S VOICE: Yes, but unfortunately they were protruding, giving her the appearance of a rabbit. (*Pause*) Her eyes seemed to be dark-brown, round eyes that dilated and flashed wonderfully while she talked.

The lights come up again. ALBERT NOBBS *and* HELEN DAWES *move. The swing door comes to life.* HELEN *is about to go through it and* ALBERT *is about to go upstairs. She stops, as if a thought has just struck her and as if she were changing her mind. She is standing in* HELEN*'s way.*

ALBERT NOBBS: I shall be off duty at three today, and if you are not engaged…

HELEN DAWES: I am off duty at three.

ALBERT NOBBS: Are you engaged?

HELEN DAWES: Well, the truth is… I was to have walked out with Joe Mackins. I can't give you a promise until I have asked him.

ALBERT NOBBS *goes upstairs and disappears into the wings.*

HELEN DAWES *is alone on stage, talking to* JOE *in the wings.*

JOE'S VOICE: He wants to walk out with you?

HELEN DAWES: He's harmless in himself, and with a very good smell of money rising out of his pockets. You seldom have a train fare upon you.

JOE'S VOICE: Why, he has never been known to walk out with man, woman or child before. Well, that's a good one! I'd like to know what he's after, but I'm not jealous; you can go with him, there's no harm in Albert. Poke him up and see what he's after, and take him into a sweet shop and bring back a box of chocolates.

40

HELEN DAWES: Do you like chocolates?

JOE'S VOICE: Where are you going to meet him?

HELEN DAWES: At the corner.

She goes over to one of the windows.

He is there already.

JOE'S VOICE: Then be off.

HELEN DAWES: You wouldn't like me to keep him waiting?

JOE'S VOICE: Oh, dear no, not for Joe, not for Joseph, if he knows it. (JOE *lilts the song*)

HELEN DAWES: You won't peach upon me to the others, will you?

THE WALK IN THE STREET

There are three shop signs in the street: a confectioner's, a jeweller's and a draper's. ALBERT NOBBS *is sitting waiting on a bench.*

HELEN DAWES *joins him.*

HELEN DAWES: Were you afraid I wasn't coming?

ALBERT NOBBS (*very shyly*): Not really.

HELEN DAWES *pouts slightly. This seems a stupid answer to her. Silence. They sit down on the bench. An embarrassed pause.* HELEN DAWES *looks round her and stands up. She reads the shop sign: O'Toole, Confectioner.*

ALBERT NOBBS: Do you like chocolates?

HELEN DAWES: Something to nibble at will help the time away.

ALBERT NOBBS'S VOICE: A shilling or one and sixpence will see me through it.

They are looking in the window of the confectioner's shop.

HELEN DAWES: Might I have one of those large, pictured boxes?

ALBERT NOBBS: Yes... I'm afraid they'll cost a lot.

HELEN DAWES *shrugs her shoulders disdainfully.* ALBERT NOBBS *hastens to add:*

ALBERT NOBBS: Oh, I'll buy you two, Helen. One to pass the time with and another to take home.

HELEN DAWES: I love chocolates. Of course you will say, Albert, that they make you fat. But I don't mind; if you had to go without...

ALBERT NOBBS'S VOICE: Three and sixpence! How dreadful!

HELEN DAWES: Joe likes chocolates too, but he prefers cigars. That's natural for a man, isn't it?

ALBERT NOBBS'S VOICE: Yes, but she has expensive tastes. If every walk is to cost me three and sixpence...

GEORGE MOORE'S VOICE: In fact, there wouldn't be a lot left for the home in six months' time. And

Albert fell to calculating how much it would cost her if they were to walk out once a week.

ALBERT NOBBS'S VOICE: Three fours are twelve and four sixpences are two shillings, fourteen shillings a month, twice that is twenty-eight; twenty-eight shillings a month if Helen wants two boxes a week. At that rate I'd be spending sixteen pounds sixteen shillings a year.

In the meantime HELEN DAWES *has wandered off and is gazing into the shop windows. They come to the jeweller's.*

ALBERT NOBB'S VOICE: Lord amassy! But perhaps Helen won't want two boxes of chocolates every time we go out together.

ALBERT NOBBS *suddenly realizes that* HELEN DAWES *is looking in the jeweller's window, and tries to avert her attention.*

ALBERT NOBBS: Look, Helen – that cyclist only just managed to escape a tram car. He gave a sudden wriggle.

HELEN DAWES *comes over, happily.*

GEORGE MOORE'S VOICE: But Albert was always unlucky.

HELEN DAWES: Oh! I've been wishing this long while for a bicycle, Albert!

She goes back to the jeweller's.

What pretty bangles!

GEORGE MOORE'S VOICE: For a moment Albert's heart seemed to stand still.

ALBERT NOBBS *tries once again to lead her away from the shop windows.*

ALBERT NOBBS: Come, Helen, I want to show you the north side of the city.

HELEN DAWES: I have little taste for the meaner parts, and I wonder what you can find to interest you in those streets.

ALBERT NOBBS: They're so pleasant! and there are all those small newspaper and tobacco shops.

Their daily takings are very good. You might take as much as four pounds a week, two hundred pounds a year! And if you add on the sweets... That would be even better. They would make a very pretty home, with a parlour...

HELEN DAWES *arrives at the draper's shop.*

HELEN DAWES: I would like a pair of six-button gloves. If I had a silk kerchief and some new stockings and shoes, I would wear them next Thursday, if you invited me to walk with you, Albert.

They walk off.

HELEN DAWES *immediately returns to her conversation with* JOE. *She is making a show of doing some housework, but most of the time she stops at the swing door to talk to Joe.*

HELEN DAWES: Until I remembered suddenly that he had invested his savings in house property. Did you know that, Joe? Could those be his houses? All his own? Who knows? I reckon that he is a richer man than anybody believes him to be, but he is a mean one. The idea of his thinking twice about a box of chocolates! I'll show him, I said to myself, and it seemed to me that the time had come to speak of bangles. For three pounds I could have a pretty one, I told him, and I even said: one that it will be a real pleasure to wear; it will always remind me of you.

JOE'S VOICE: How did he take that?

HELEN DAWES: He coughed up. And I felt that I had "got him".

JOE'S VOICE: So he parted easily. But I say, old girl, since he's coughing up so easily you might bring me something back; a briar-wood pipe and a pound or two of tobacco, that's the least you might obtain for me.

HELEN DAWES: To get those I would have to ask Albert for money.

JOE'S VOICE: And why shouldn't you? It's the first quid that's hard to get; every time after it's like shelling peas.

HELEN: Do you think he's that far gone on me?

JOE'S VOICE: Well, don't you? Why should he give you these things if he wasn't? (*Pause*) What do you think of him?

HELEN DAWES: It's hard to say. I have walked out with many a man before but never with one like Albert Nobbs.

JOE'S VOICE: In what way is he different?

HELEN DAWES: There's a sort of slackness about him.

JOE'S VOICE (*amused*): You mean he doesn't pull you about?

HELEN DAWES: There's something of that in it, but that isn't the whole of it. I've been out before with men that didn't pull me about, but he seems to have something on his mind, and half the time he's thinking.

JOE'S VOICE: Well, what does that matter, so long as there is coin in his pockets?

HELEN DAWES: I don't like it. I don't want to go out any more with Albert. I'm tired of the job.

JOE'S VOICE: Next time you go out with him, work him up a bit and see what he is made of; just see if there's a sting in him or if he is not better than a capon.

HELEN DAWES: A capon? And what is a capon?

JOE'S VOICE: A capon is a castrated fowl. He may be like one.

HELEN DAWES: You think that, do you? I shall get the truth of the matter. It does seem odd that he should be willing to buy me presents and not want to kiss me. In fact, it is more than odd. I might as well go out with my mother. It may be as you say. Or is it a blind?... some other girl that he...

I'm beginning to feel ugly towards him. He must know that I'm partial to you.

MRS BAKER *comes from the kitchens, followed by* HELEN DAWES, *who has taken a pile of plates from the sideboard.* ALBERT NOBBS *comes downstairs with a pile of sheets. During the following speeches they look at each other over* MRS BAKER, *who doesn't understand a thing, and exits.* HELEN DAWES *stays for a moment, legs apart, in front of the wing door, and then goes out.* ALBERT NOBBS *goes upstairs, puts her sheets down outside one of the doors in the backcloth, then comes down again slowly for the rest of the scene.*

HELEN DAWES: It really is a bit much.

ALBERT NOBBS'S VOICE: I know that Helen is carrying on with Joe Mackins. I even suspect that some of the money I have given her has gone to purchase pipes and tobacco for him.

GEORGE MOORE'S VOICE: A certain shrewdness is not incompatible with innocence.

HELEN DAWES: Good morning, Mrs Baker.

MRS BAKER: Yesterday, Helen, you went off duty before you'd dried the glasses.

HELEN DAWES: I did, Mrs Baker? I'm sorry, Mrs Baker.

ALBERT NOBBS'S VOICE: It's better for her to have her fling before than after marriage.

HELEN DAWES: I can't see what he is after.

Both voices can be heard simultaneously.

ALBERT NOBBS'S VOICE: She might hanker for children. I feel that I would like a child as well as another. But if Joe Mackins was the father, I foresee trouble.

HELEN DAWES: In any case, I've had enough; I prefer Joe.

ALBERT NOBBS *goes up to her favourite place on the chair in the middle of the staircase. The lights dim.*

ALBERT NOBBS: I would prefer another father. (*Pause*) Almost any other. (*Pause*) Of course, there would be the expense of the lying-in. (*Pause*) But how should I tell Helen? Blurt it out? – I've something to tell you, Helen. I'm not a man, but a woman like yourself. (*Pause*) No, that wouldn't do. How did Hubert manage? If I had only asked her, I should have been spared all this trouble. (*Pause*) But she has a violent temper. (*Pause*) Though after her first outburst she might quieten down, when she begins to see that it might be very much to her advantage to accept the situation. (*Pause*) But if she were to cut up rough and do me an injury! She might call the neighbours in, or the policeman, who'd take us both to the station. I'd have to return to Liverpool or to Manchester.

GEORGE MOORE'S VOICE: Her thoughts wandered onto the morning boat.

ALEC'S VOICE: One of the advantages of Dublin, Your Honour, is that one can get out of it as easily as any other city.

ALBERT NOBBS'S VOICE: On the other hand, if I take the straight course, Helen might promise not to tell, but she might break her promise. What a hue and cry! Life in Morrison's Hotel would be unendurable. (*Pause*) If it hadn't been for that flea I wouldn't be in this mess.

ALEC'S VOICE: It was a different sort of girl altogether that she would have needed.

GEORGE MOORE'S VOICE: But she liked Helen, with her way of standing on a doorstep, her legs a little apart, jawing a tradesman, and she'd stand up to Mrs Baker and to the chef himself. She liked the way Helen's eyes lighted up when a thought came into her mind; her cheery laugh warmed Albert's heart as nothing else did. Before she met Helen she often feared her heart was growing cold.

ALBERT NOBBS'S VOICE: I might try the world over and not find one that would run the shop I have in mind as well as Helen.

THE BREAK

Enter HELEN DAWES, *coming downstairs.*

HELEN DAWES: Are you dreaming, Albert, or are you dozing?

ALBERT NOBBS: I was thinking…

HELEN DAWES: If we went out together this evening, we might go for a walk on the banks of the Dodder.

ALBERT NOBBS: Oh, I should like that.

ALBERT NOBBS *hurries up the stairs, removes her apron and takes her jacket from a peg.* HELEN DAWES *sends her apron flying and snatches up a little cape. All these movements must be rapid. Both of them pass through the revolving door as if caught up in the movement of a top, and then immediately re-enter. They have come back from their walk: they have quarrelled and are furious. During the next scene the two chambermaids are always in the place where* ALBERT NOBBS *ought to be, facing* HELEN DAWES. HELEN DAWES *is thus encircled by two women Alberts and one man Albert. As for* ALBERT NOBBS *herself, she is encircled by three Helens by this mirror game and by* trompe l'oeil; *refusal and incomprehension are shown.*

ALBERT NOBBS: I beseech you not to cast me off. If I've been stupid today it's because I'm tired of the work in the hotel. I shall be different when we get to Lisdoonvarna: we both want a change of air: there's nothing like the salt water and the cliffs of Clare to put new spirits into a man. You will be different and I'll be different – everything will be different.

HELEN DAWES *shakes her head.*

Don't say no, Helen; don't say no. I've looked forward to this week in Lisdoonvarna. I have already engaged the lodgings, we shall have to pay for them, and there's the new suit of clothes that have just come back from the tailor's. I've looked forward to wearing it, walking with you in the strand, the waves crashing up into the cliffs, with green fields among them, I've been told! We shall see the ships passing and wonder whither they are going. I've bought three neckties and some new shirts, and what good will these be to me if you'll not come to Lisdoonvarna with me?

HELEN DAWES: Oh, don't talk to me about Lisdoonvarna. I'm not going to Lisdoonvarna with you.

ALBERT NOBBS: But what is to become of the hat I have ordered for you – the hat with the big feather in it? And I've bought stockings and shoes for you. Tell me, what shall I do with these, and with the gloves? Oh, the waste of money and the heart-breaking! What shall I do with the hat?

HELEN DAWES: You can leave the hat with me.

ALBERT NOBBS: And the stockings?

HELEN DAWES: Yes, you can leave the stockings.

ALBERT NOBBS: And the shoes?

HELEN DAWES: Yes, you can leave the shoes too.

ALBERT NOBBS: Yet you won't go to Lisdoonvarna with me?

HELEN DAWES: No, I'll not go to Lisdoonvarna with you.

ALBERT NOBBS: But you'll take the presents?

HELEN DAWES: It was to please you that I said I would take them, because I thought it would be some satisfaction to you to know that they wouldn't be wasted.

ALBERT NOBBS: Not wasted? You'll wear them when you go out with Joe Mackins.

HELEN DAWES: Oh well, keep your presents.

ALBERT NOBBS: We cannot part like this! Let us talk things over and do nothing foolish. You see, I had set my heart on driving on an outside car to the Broadstone with you, and catching a train, and the train going into lovely country, arriving at a place we had never seen, with cliffs, and the sunset behind the cliffs...

HELEN DAWES: You've told me all that before. I'm not going to Lisdoonvarna with you. And if that is all you had to say to me...

ALBERT NOBBS: But there's much more, Helen. I haven't told you about the shop yet.

HELEN DAWES: Yes, you have told me all there is to say about the shop; you've been talking about that shop for the last three months.

ALBERT NOBBS: But Helen, it was only yesterday that I got a letter saying that they had had another offer for the shop, and that they could give me only till Monday morning to close with them; if the lease isn't signed by then we've lost the shop.

HELEN DAWES: But what makes you think that the shop will be a success? Many shops promise well in the beginning and fade away till they don't get a customer a day.

ALBERT NOBBS: Our shop won't be like that, I know it won't. We shall be able to make a great success of that shop, and people will be coming to see us, and they will be having tea with us in the parlour, and they'll envy us, saying that never have two people had such luck as we have had. And our wedding will be…

HELEN DAWES: Will be what?

ALBERT NOBBS: A great wonder.

HELEN DAWES: A great wonder indeed. But I'm not going to wed you, Albert Nobbs.

ALBERT NOBBS goes back to the bench. A simultaneous scene:

JOE'S VOICE: What happened on the walk?

HELEN DAWES: Phew! I've broken with Albert. It was in the hope that the river's bank might tempt him into a confidence that I suggested that we might spend the evening by the Dodder.

ALBERT NOBBS: The river's bank might tempt me into a confidence.

HELEN DAWES: But he said nothing. He seemed to be afraid.

ALBERT NOBBS: The silence round us... the river flowing over its muddy bottom without ripple or eddy... I felt as if I were choking.

JOE'S VOICE: And did he not speak on the way there?

HELEN DAWES: Not a word.

JOE'S VOICE: But tell me – what happened?

HELEN DAWES: There is nothing to tell... It was all very simple... you'll see.

HELEN DAWES *gets dressed again and goes and sits down beside* ALBERT NOBBS *for the following flashback.*

THE BANKS OF THE DODDER

HELEN DAWES: What are you thinking of?

ALBERT NOBBS (*startled*): Of you, dear; and how pleasant it is to be sitting with you.

The sound of laughter, and of people passing.

A LAD'S VOICE: I'll see if you have any lace on your drawers.

A LASS'S VOICE: You shan't.

HELEN DAWES: There's a pair that's enjoying themselves.

GEORGE MOORE'S VOICE: She looked upon this remark as fortunate, and hoped it would give Albert the courage to pursue his courtship. Albert, too, looked upon the remark as fortunate.

ALBERT NOBBS (*with an effort*): Is there lace on all women's drawers?

GEORGE MOORE'S VOICE: She hoped that this question might lead her into a confession of her sex. But the words "It's so long since I've worn any" died on her lips, and instead of speaking them...

ALBERT NOBBS: What a pity the Dodder isn't nearer Morrison's.

HELEN DAWES: Where would you have it? Flowing down Sackville Street into the Liffey? We should be lying there as thick as herrings, without room to move, and we should be unable to speak to each other without being overheard.

ALBERT NOBBS (*frightened*): I dare say you are right. But we have to be back at eleven o'clock, and it takes an hour to get there.

HELEN DAWES (*sharply*): We can go back now if you like.

ALBERT NOBBS: I'm sorry, I didn't mean that. (*Pause*) Morrison's, after all, is a good hotel for servants. Is the Dodder pretty all the way down to the sea?

HELEN DAWES: There are woods as far as Dartry – the Dartry Dye Works, don't you know them? But I don't think there are any very pretty spots. You know Ring's End, don't you?

ALBERT NOBBS: No.

HELEN DAWES: Some Sundays ago I saw a large three-masted vessel by the quays.

ALBERT NOBBS: You were there with Joe Mackins, weren't you?

HELEN DAWES: Well, what if I was?

ALBERT NOBBS: Only this: that I don't think it is usual for a girl to keep company with two chaps, and I thought…

HELEN DAWES: Now, what did you think?

ALBERT NOBBS: That you didn't care for me well enough for…

HELEN DAWES: For what? You know we've been going out for three months, and it doesn't seem natural to keep talking always, never wanting to put your arm round a girl's waist.

ALBERT NOBBS: I suppose Joe isn't like me, then?

HELEN DAWES *gives a scornful little laugh.*

But isn't the time for kissing when one is wedded?

HELEN DAWES: This is the first time you've said anything about marriage.

ALBERT NOBBS: But I thought there had always been an understanding between us, and it's only now I can tell you what I have to offer.

GEORGE MOORE'S VOICE: The words were well chosen.

HELEN DAWES: Tell me about it.

ALBERT NOBBS: Well, the shop, you know, could bring in a good income. We might make as much as four pounds a week – two hundred pounds a year! We could make a little more, especially if I now and then got jobs in hotels or even – why not – in private houses. I have enough connections. We would have a very pretty home. I foresee a pair of candlesticks, or perhaps you don't like... a round mirror...

HELEN DAWES (*bored*): All you say about the shop is right enough, but it isn't a very great compliment to a girl.

ALBERT NOBBS: What? To ask her to marry?

HELEN DAWES: Well, no, not if you haven't kissed her first.

ALBERT NOBBS (*whispering*): Don't speak so loud, I'm sure that couple heard what you said, for they went away laughing.

HELEN DAWES: I don't care whether they laughed or cried. You don't want to kiss me, do you? And I don't want to marry a man who isn't in love with me.

ALBERT NOBBS: But I do want to kiss you.

ALBERT NOBBS *leans over and kisses* HELEN DAWES *on both cheeks.*

Now you can't say I haven't kissed you, can you?

HELEN DAWES: You don't call that kissing, do you?

ALBERT NOBBS: But how do you wish me to kiss you, Helen?

HELEN DAWES: Well, you are an innocent! People kiss on the lips!

ALBERT NOBBS: I'm not used to that.

HELEN DAWES: Because you're not in love.

ALBERT NOBBS: Not in love? I loved my old nurse very much, but I never wished to kiss her like that.

HELEN DAWES: So you put me in the same class with your old nurse! Well, after that!… Come (*taking pity upon* ALBERT NOBBS *for a moment*) – are you or are you not in love with me?

ALBERT NOBBS: I love you deeply, Helen.

HELEN DAWES: You love me? The men who have walked out with me were in love with me.

ALBERT NOBBS: In love? I'm sure I love you.

HELEN DAWES: I like men to be in love with me.

ALBERT NOBBS: But that's like the animals, Helen.

HELEN DAWES: Whatever put that nonsense in your head? I've had enough. I'm going home.

ALBERT NOBBS: You're angry with me, Helen?

HELEN DAWES: Angry? No, I'm not angry with you. You're a fool of a man, that's all.

ALBERT NOBBS: But if you think me a fool of a man, why have we been keeping company for the last three months? You didn't always think me a fool of a man, did you?

HELEN DAWES: Yes, I did.

ALBERT NOBBS: Then what reason did you have for choosing my company?

HELEN DAWES: Oh, you bother me, asking reasons for everything.

ALBERT NOBBS: But why did you make me love you?

HELEN DAWES: Well, if I did, what of it? And as for walking out with you, you won't have to complain of that any more.

ALBERT NOBBS: You don't mean, Helen, that we are never going to walk out again?

HELEN DAWES: Yes, I do.

ALBERT NOBBS: You mean that for the future you'll be walking out with Joe Mackins?

HELEN DAWES: That's my business.

ALBERT NOBBS: I beseech you to change your mind.

HELEN DAWES *walks off, and comes back to* JOE.

HELEN DAWES (*to* JOE): His old nurse! Just imagine, Joe Mackins! "That's like the animals…" Let him keep his shop… There! that's what happened!

She takes off her hat, goes and fetches her apron, puts it on as she passes through the swing doors and disappears.

THE MEETING WITH THE PROSTITUTE

ALBERT NOBBS *is in the street. Enter a prostitute, continuing a conversation with one of her colleagues, whom we cannot see.*

KITTY MACCAN: It was almost a love dream.

ALBERT NOBBS'S VOICE: They at least are women. Whereas I am only a perhapser…

ALBERT NOBBS: If I speak to her, she'll expect me to… (*Pause*) Almost a love dream? What are you two women talking about?

KITTY MACCAN: My friend here was telling me of a dream she had last night.

ALBERT NOBBS: A dream? And what was her dream about?

KITTY MACCAN: She was telling me that she was better than a love dream; now do you think she is, sir?

ALBERT NOBBS: What is your name?

KITTY MacCAN: Kitty MacCan.

ALBERT NOBBS: It's odd we've never met before.

KITTY MacCAN: We're not often this way.

ALBERT NOBBS: And where do you walk usually – of an evening?

KITTY MacCAN: In Grafton Street, or down by College Green; sometimes we cross the river.

ALBERT NOBBS: To walk in Sackville Street… That must be difficult for you…

KITTY MacCAN: I hope you are not one of those who think that we should wash clothes in a nunnery for nothing?

ALBERT NOBBS: I'm a waiter in Morrison's Hotel.

KITTY MacCAN: Is the money good in your hotel? I've heard that you get as much as half a crown for carrying up a cup of tea. I – when I was but a girl, it was not cups of tea they asked of me for less than that. But you are not interested in my story… (*Pause*) The river is pretty all the way down to the sea. There are woods as far as Dartry. (*Pause*) Do you know Ring's End?

ALBERT NOBBS: No.

KITTY MacCAN: Nor do I. (*Pause*) There are big boats, three-masters, so they say… the waves breaking against the cliffs – the green meadows atop the cliffs – so they say!… Large vessels with every stitch of canvas spread. (*Pause*) You wonder where they are going! (*Pause*) Do you know Connemara, sir?

ALBERT NOBBS: No.

KITTY MacCAN. They say it is a very pretty place, with fishing boats, and tall cliffs, too, full of sea-gulls. When you are up upon them you can see the sun sinking into the sea... (*Pause*) Are you very unhappy?

ALBERT NOBBS: It doesn't matter about me.

KITTY MacCAN: Perhaps I can help you out of your sorrow, if only for a little while. Things do not always go so well for me, you know... I have only three and sixpence left out of the last money I received, and my rent will be due tomorrow. I daren't return home without a gentleman, my landlady will be at me, and the best time of the night is going by... You're a waiter, aren't you? I've forgotten which hotel you said.

ALBERT NOBBS *doesn't answer.*

I'm afraid I'm taking you out of your way.

ALBERT NOBBS: No, you aren't; all ways are the same to me.

KITTY MacCAN: Well, they aren't to me. I must get some money tonight.

ALBERT NOBBS: I'll give you some money.

KITTY MacCAN: But you won't come home with me?

They stand facing each other, not moving, while GEORGE MOORE'S VOICE *is heard.*

GEORGE MOORE'S VOICE: But if they were to go home together her sex would be discovered. Though what did it matter if it were discovered? Albert asked herself. And the temptation came again to go home with this woman, to lie in her arms and tell the story that had been locked up so many years. They could both have a good cry together, and what matter would it be to the woman as long as she got the money she desired? She didn't want a man; it was money she was after, money that meant bread and board to her. She seems a kind, nice girl, Albert said to herself.

KITTY MacCAN *suddenly sees one of her friends.*

KITTY MacCAN: Oh, there is James. Excuse me.

She runs over and calls to him, then returns.

KITTY MacCAN: I'm sorry, but I've just met an old friend. Another evening, perhaps.

ALBERT NOBBS *puts her hand in her pocket, wanting to pay the woman with some silver for her company, but she has already gone.*

ALBERT NOBBS: I have let all my chances go by me... Is it better to be casual, as these girls are, or to have a husband that you cannot get rid of? This is an idle question.

ALBERT NOBBS *goes back to the hotel.* MRS BAKER *is at her table.* ALBERT NOBBS *takes off her overcoat and puts on her apron. She is sad, depressed, tired.*

MRS BAKER (*after looking at her indicator board*): It's 34, Albert.

ALBERT NOBBS *goes up to 34 and comes down very quickly, passing in front of* MRS BAKER.

MRS BAKER: What was it?

ALBERT NOBBS: It was for the kitchen, Mrs Baker.

ALBERT NOBBS *is ready to dash into the kitchen.*

MRS BAKER: Leave it, Albert; you can go upstairs.

ALBERT NOBBS *walks off, disappointed.*

MRS BAKER (*calling*): Helen Dawes, for 34.

HELEN DAWES *comes out.* ALBERT NOBBS *waits for her at the bottom of the stairs. They pass each other.*

ALBER NOBBS: Are you going to pass me by without speaking again, Helen?

HELEN DAWES: We talked enough last night. There's nothing more to say.

HELEN DAWES *goes up, and into 34.* ALBERT NOBBS *goes and sits on his chair.* HELEN DAWES *comes down again and exits. Through the swing door* JOE *can be heard guffawing and saying:*

JOE'S VOICE: I loved my old nurse, but I never thought of kissing her like that.

Sound of plates falling with a great clatter.

MRS BAKER: What has come over you, Joe Mackins? I shall keep that back out of your wages.

ALBERT NOBBS: That is well deserved!

ALBERT NOBBS *is alone on stage in her usual place, her napkin over her shoulder. The lights go down and the maids' voices are heard like a flight of birds. The two ghost-chambermaids can be seen between the doors.*

HOUSEMAIDS' VOICES: Well, Albert! You cannot get a word out of him today.

–"I loved my old nurse" (*giggling*)

–Be quiet.

–Be quiet, Kathy.

–After all, he loves the girl, there's nothing to laugh about.

–That Helen! Why should she have kept company with Albert if she didn't mean to wed him?

–Look at him; there is no more colour in his face than is in my duster.

–I poured out a glass of wine for him that was left over, but he put it away.

–And the shop he was offering her – that was no small thing.

–A newspaper and tobacco shop, that can hardly fail to prosper, especially with the sweets… Helen will live to regret her cruelty.

–I would rather say treachery.

–Alice is right; Helen's face is full of treachery.

All these voices must follow each other very quickly, or rather all talk at once, like the hubbub of a recreation ground heard over the background of the music of an Irish reel.

GEORGE MOORE'S VOICE: And they dispersed in different directions, flicking their dusters.

From now on, ALBERT NOBBS *spends almost all her time on her chair on the landing.*

GEORGE MOORE'S VOICE: Almost any one of the women in the hotel would have married Albert out of pity for her. But there was no heart in Albert for another adventure, nor any thought in her for anything but her work.

ALBERT NOBBS: I shall never see Lisdoonvarna, nor the shop with the two counters, one for the tobacco, cigarettes and matches, and the other for the sweets. It only existed in my mind – a thought, a dream.

GEORGE MOORE'S VOICE: Yet it had possessed her completely; the parlour behind the shop that she had furnished and refurnished, hanging a round mirror above the mantelpiece, hanging the walls with a pretty colourful paper... With curtains about the windows, two armchairs on either side of the hearth, one in green and one in red velvet, for herself and Helen... There had never been anything in her life but a few dreams, and henceforth there would be not even dreams... She had been unlucky from her birth; she was a bastard...

ALBERT NOBBS *nods her head; this last sentence prompts her to speak:*

ALBERT NOBBS: My old nurse and I had to go out charring. Mr Congreve had a French mistress, and if it hadn't been for Bessie Lawrence I might have thrown myself in the Thames, but I shall never throw myself into this Dublin river. Perhaps because it is not my own river. If one wishes to drown oneself it had better be in one's own country. But what is the difference? For a perhapser like myself, all countries are the same. (*Pause*)

GEORGE MOORE'S VOICE: Only to Hubert Page could she confide the misfortune that had befallen her.

ALBERT NOBBS *listens to* GEORGE MOORE'S VOICE *and still seems to be answering it.*

ALBERT NOBBS: Now with Hubert, the three of us might set up together. A happy family we might make. Two women in men's clothes and one in petticoats. But if Hubert were willing, his wife might not be. Though she might be dead, and Hubert on the lookout for another helpmate.

GEORGE MOORE'S VOICE: And from the moment that she foresaw herself as Hubert's future wife, her life began to expand itself more eagerly than ever in watching for tips. As the months went by, and the years, she remembered, with increasing bitterness, that she had wasted nearly twenty pounds on Helen, that cruel, heartless girl. She took to counting her money in her room at night. The half-crowns were folded up in brown-paper packets, the half-sovereigns in blue, the rare sovereigns were in pink paper, and all these little packets were hidden away in different corners... A sense of almost happiness awoke in her the day she discovered herself to be again as rich as she was before she met Helen. Richer by twenty-five pounds twelve and sixpence. Her eyes roved over the garret floor in search of a plank that might be lifted.

ALBERT NOBBS: Hubert... A wandering fellow like him might easily run out of money and return to Morrison's Hotel to borrow from me. If he came back he might threaten to publish my secret if I didn't give him money to keep quiet. No... that is an ugly thought... But even so...

GEORGE MOORE'S VOICE: As time went on, a dread of Hubert took possession of her.

MRS BAKER *enters, looks at a part of the wall and says to herself:*

MRS BAKER: That could do with a good spring clean.

She notices ALBERT NOBBS.

Ah, you are there, Albert... By the way, I cannot think what has become of Hubert Page; we've not had news of him for a long time. Have you heard from him, Albert?

ALBERT NOBBS: Why should you think, ma'am, that I hear from him?

MRS BAKER (*displeased with Albert's tone*): I only asked.

They are speaking with their backs turned to one another.

ALBERT NOBBS (*mumbling as he goes out*): A wandering fellow...

They go out, each on her own side. ALBERT NOBBS *picks up a pair of shoes and starts cleaning them with tired, mechanical movements. The lights go down. Death merely halts her movements and freezes her sulky expression on her face.*

ALBERT'S DEATH

GEORGE MOORE'S VOICE: Albert remained at Morrison's Hotel till she died.

ALEC'S VOICE: An easy death I hope it was, Your Honour, for if any poor creature deserved an easy one it was Albert herself.

GEORGE MOORE'S VOICE: You, mean, Alec, that the disappointed man suffers less at parting with this world than the happy one? Maybe you're right.

ALEC'S VOICE: That is as it may be, Your Honour.

GEORGE MOORE'S VOICE: Albert woke one morning hardly able to breathe. When the maidservant came to make the bed she ran off again to fetch a cup of tea. It was plain that Albert could not eat or drink, and it was almost plain that she was dying, but the maidservant did not like to alarm the hotel and contented herself with saying he'd better see the doctor tomorrow. She was up early in the morning, and on going to Albert's room she found the waiter asleep, breathing heavily. An hour later, Albert was dead. (*Pause*) Which did not seem natural, but when the doctor came down with his report that Albert was a woman, this put all thought of the cause of death out of everybody's mind. Never before or since was Morrison's Hotel agog as it was that morning. The men giggled over their glasses, and the women pondered over their cups of tea; the men questioned the women, and the women questioned the men.

HUBERT'S RETURN

A pretty spring light floods the stage, coming through all the doors and windows, but leaving some patches of soft shadow.

Enter HUBERT PAGE, *with his paint pots and brushes.*

HUBERT PAGE: Is anyone there?

He goes over to the swing doors and leaves his equipment in the middle of them. He goes into the kitchen. During the whole of this sequence the doors swing gently and the conversation in the kitchen can be heard. ALBERT NOBBS, *dead, is in her usual place, on the chair halfway up the staircase. As if she were pinned onto the backcloth, with her napkin over her shoulder, sitting facing the audience, her legs a little apart, holding on her knees, with one hand, the pair of shoes she was polishing... In this soft spring light, the door swings as if wafted on the breeze of the voices.*

HUBERT PAGE: Good morning, all!

VOICES: –Good morning, Hubert!

    –Why, it's Hubert Page!

HUBERT PAGE: How is Albert Nobbs?

DIFFERENT VOICES: Albert Nobbs! Don't you know?

HUBERT PAGE: How should I know? I've only just come back to Dublin. What is there to know?

VOICES: Don't you ever read the papers?

HUBERT PAGE: Read the papers?

VOICE: Then you haven't heard that Albert Nobbs is dead?

HUBERT PAGE: No, I haven't heard of it. I'm sorry for him, but after all, men die; there's nothing wonderful in that, is there?

VOICE: No, but if you had read the papers you'd have learnt that Albert wasn't a man at all, he was a woman.

HUBERT PAGE: Albert Nobbs a woman!

DIFFERENT VOICES (*at the same time*):—So you never heard?
    —She courted Helen.
    —A real broken heart.
    —Helen preferred Joe Mackins.

HUBERT PAGE: If you all speak together, I shall never understand it. Albert Nobbs a woman!

A SCULLION'S VOICE: The biggest deception in the whole world.

HUBERT PAGE: So Helen went away with Joe Mackins?

VOICE: Yes, and they don't seem to get on very well together.

VOICE: And the hundreds of pounds that Albert left behind...

VOICE: Nearly a hundred in ready money...

VOICE: Much more! Rolled up in paper.

VOICE: A great scoop it was for the Government.

VOICE: I think that the real reason at the start was that she would be getting better wages as a man than as a woman.

DIFFERENT VOICES (*rather low*): Everyone knows that.

VOICE: Now I come to think of it, Mr Page, it's you that should be knowing better than anybody else what Albert's sex was like. Didn't you sleep with her once?

HUBERT PAGE: Oh! I fell asleep the moment my head was on the pillow. If you remember rightly, I was that tired Mrs Baker hadn't the heart to turn me out of the hotel. I'd been working ten, twelve, fourteen hours that day. When Albert took me up to his room I fell asleep right away, and I left in the morning before he was awake. A woman, I just can't believe it. How ever did she manage to play such a part for so long?

MRS BAKER *enters during this speech and is delighted to discover* HUBERT PAGE'*s paint pots and brushes.*

MRS BAKER: Mr Page! Come over here, do.

HUBERT PAGE: Good morning, Mrs Baker.

MRS BAKER: Good morning, Hubert. Have they told you the news?

HUBERT PAGE: It is quite extraordinary, Mrs Baker. It is also very sad that poor Albert is dead.

MRS BAKER: Yes, we all liked him well. Are you going to stay the night here, Hubert?

HUBERT PAGE: If I may, Mrs Baker. I have nowhere else to stay.

HUBERT PAGE *puts his paints and brushes away in a corner while* MRS BAKER, *still talking, opens the door of* ALBERT NOBBS'*s cubby-hole.*

MRS BAKER: There's Albert's bed.

She pulls out the bed and unfolds it. HUBERT PAGE *helps her. She goes and fetches some sheets, puts them on the bed, etc. etc., while she goes on talking.*

MRS BAKER: Yes, it's an incredible story. I was only the other day telling a friend of mine such an amazing story about a woman that my friend thought it couldn't be true, it must be made up. Well, that's just it, I told her, it is made up. I've just read it. But this one is even more amazing, and yet it's true. (*Pause*) Towards the end I was beginning to observe him. He used to mumble things in a disrespectful tone; he had developed a fault which I didn't like, a way of hanging round the visitor as he was preparing to leave the hotel that almost amounted to harassment. Worse than that, a rumour had reached me that Albert's service was measured according to the tip he expected to receive. I didn't believe it, but if it had been true I would not have hesitated to have him out of the hotel in spite of the many years he had spent with us. Another thing: Albert was liked, but not by everybody. You know the little red-headed boy on the second floor, little George Moore? Well, he told me – I took him for a walk out to Bray – he told me that he was afraid of Albert. He even confided to me that Albert had tried to pick him up and kiss him one day when he was quite simply looking out of the window at the coal cart going by. Couldn't he see the child didn't like him? Ah well!… we cannot keep sentiment out of our business, Mr Baker and I, and we were very fond of Albert. He remained at Morrison's Hotel until he died. I will leave you, Hubert. Sleep well. There will be plenty of work tomorrow. I still have a few accounts to see to.

HUBERT PAGE: Goodnight, Mrs Baker. I'll see you in the morning. Thank you, Mrs Baker.

MRS BAKER: You're welcome.

MRS BAKER *goes to her table, opens her account book and stays immersed in it until the end of the play, going over and over her accounts, ruling lines, writing. Her movements are very orderly; she turns the pages of her account book, and thus lets the time pass.* HUBERT PAGE *sits down on the bed.* ALBERT NOBBS *is still at her place on her chair. It is evening.*

HUBERT PAGE: I wonder what Annie Watts was thinking of just now when she stood looking into my eyes; does she suspect me? (*Pause*) What a piece of bad luck that I shouldn't have found Albert alive. It was for her that I returned to Dublin. Now that my wife is dead, Albert and I might have set up together. One of us would have had to give up her job to attend to the shop... I would have preferred it to be me, for I'm tired of going up all those ladders. (*Pause*) I wonder what is going to be the end of my life. My husband... he might now be a different man from the one I left behind. Fifteen years makes a great difference in all of us... And the children, what will they be like now? Lily was five when I left home. She's a young woman now. Agnes was only two. She is now seventeen, still a girl... Lily's looking round, thinking of young men, and the other won't be delaying much longer... Young women are much more wide-awake than they used to be in the old days. (*Pause*) Their father could have looked after them till now, but now they are thinking of young men he won't be able to cope with them, and maybe he's wanting me too... It's odd how easy it is to forget ill-usage, and remember only the good times... The house must be there still... I recall it all: the pictures on the wall, the chairs I sat in, the coverlets on the beds, everything. But how would I return home? Pack up my things and go dressed as a man to the house? No, they wouldn't understand. I must put on woman's clothes again. (*Pause*) But what story would I tell them?

ALEC'S VOICE: But sure 'twas an easy story to tell.

GEORGE MOORE'S VOICE: Really? Well then, Alec, what story should she have told them?

ALEC'S VOICE: In these parts, a woman who left her husband and returned to him after fifteen years would say she was taken away by the little people whilst wandering in a wood.

GEORGE MOORE'S VOICE: Do you think she'd be believed?

ALEC'S VOICE: Why shouldn't she, Your Honour? A woman that marries another woman, and lives happily with her, isn't a natural woman; there must be something of a fairy in her.

The lights on the stage dim. It is just possible to make out MRS BAKER, *at her table,* ALBERT NOBBS, *in her place halfway up the stairs, with the shoes to be cleaned on one knee and the napkin over her shoulder, and* HUBERT PAGE, *dreaming, sitting on the bed. The two chambermaids pull the curtains, just as they would pull curtains over a window, and a woman's voice sings, in Gaelic,* 'Róisín dubh'.

Printed in Great Britain
by Amazon.co.uk, Ltd.,
Marston Gate.